Knights

Stephanie Turnbull

Designed by Helen Wood

Illustrated by Ian McNee

Cover illustration by Ian Jackson

Knights consultant: Dr. Abigail Wheatley

Reading consultant: Alison Kelly,
Roehampton University

Contents

Charge!

Knights were fighting men who rode into battle on horses. They lived in Europe more than 500 years ago.

These men are dressed to look like knights charging at an enemy.

All knights were very good riders. They owned many different horses.

Different knights

Knights were always rich men.
They were usually the sons
of other knights.

This old
painting
shows a knight
riding into battle.

The richest knights were kings. They lived in huge castles.

Other knights worked for kings and fought in battles with them.

Some knights ran hospitals where they cared for sick people.

Troubadours were knights who sang and wrote poems.

Knights were supposed to be polite, honest and well-behaved at all times.

In training

It took many years to learn to be a knight. First, boys became pages when they were six or seven.

Pages went to work for other rich families.

They learned to ride horses and clean stables.

Later, they became squires for knights.

A squire learned to hit a target with a long lance.

If he was too slow, the target swung around and hit him.

In this old painting, a squire is helping his master dress for battle.

Becoming a knight

When many squires were about 18 years old, they became knights in a special ceremony.

1. A squire stayed up all night praying before the ceremony.

2. The next morning, servants helped him dress as a knight.

3. He was tapped with a sword, which made him a knight.

4. The new knight was given a sword and other presents.

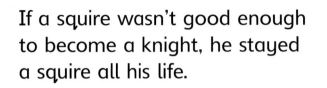

If a squire wasn't good enough to become a knight, he stayed a squire all his life.

This old painting shows a squire being made a knight after a battle.

What to wear

Knights wore clothes that helped to protect them in battle.

Early knights had tunics of metal rings called chain mail.

This man is making chain mail. A finished tunic hangs behind him.

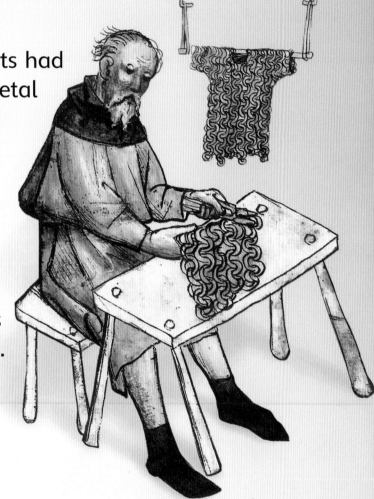

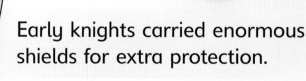

Early knights carried enormous shields for extra protection.

10

Later, knights wore metal plates over their chain mail.

They had a hard helmet that covered their whole head.

Knights usually carried a shield, a sword and a knife.

This is what a knight might have looked like 500 years ago.

Into battle

Kings sometimes went to war with each other. They sent armies of knights to fight battles for them.

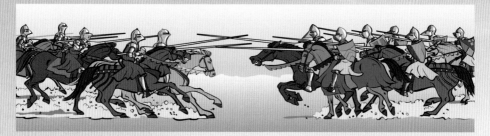

First, the two armies of knights charged at each other with pointed lances.

Some knights broke their lances and others were knocked off their horses.

Men who weren't hurt continued fighting on foot with swords and knives.

These men are taking part in a pretend battle, dressed as knights.

13

Attacking a castle

Often an army attacked an enemy castle and tried to take it over.

Soldiers in the castle fired arrows at the attackers, or poured boiling water on them.

Knights climbed tall ladders to get into the castle.

Battering rams were used to smash big holes in the walls and doors.

Soldiers fired rocks at the walls to break them down.

15

At a joust

Knights often fought each other in exciting contests called jousts.

People came to watch and cheer.

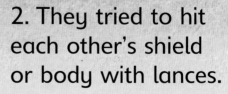

1. In a joust, two knights thundered towards each other.

2. They tried to hit each other's shield or body with lances.

Sometimes knights tried jousting in boats.

These men are putting on a modern jousting display, dressed as knights.

3. Often one of the knights was pushed off his horse.

4. Then the knights fought on foot until one was the winner.

Castle life

Rich knights had enormous castles with wide courtyards.

The tall, main tower was for the knight and his guests.

Servants lived and worked in the courtyard.

There were stables for horses and kennels for dogs.

All the meals were cooked in a kitchen in the courtyard.

Servants fetched water from a deep well.

19

Knights at home

A rich knight lived with his family, his squire, poorer knights and lots of servants.

The knight and his family had the best rooms in the castle.

The knight spent the day giving orders and counting money.

Women sewed, made tapestries or listened to songs.

In the evening, the knight invited friends to a huge feast.

Some castles had walled gardens where people sat or walked.

When a knight was away, his wife looked after the castle.

Hunting

Knights enjoyed hunting animals on the land around their homes.

In this old picture a knight aims at birds with a bow and arrow.

Knights liked to hunt wild boars, which were very fierce and hard to catch.

Knights often went on a big hunt with
their families, friends and servants.

If the dogs smelled a deer, they chased
after it. The hunters raced along behind.

Men tried to shoot the deer with arrows.
The chase could go on for hours.

Fighting abroad

Knights called crusaders fought wars called Crusades against people of other religions.

This old painting shows a knight in a black helmet setting off with his army to fight in a Crusade.

Many crusaders fought in the Middle East.
They built this castle called Sidon in Lebanon.

Lots of violent battles were fought in the Middle East.

Finally the crusaders were defeated, so they went home.

Knights brought back lots of beautiful things from the Crusades.

Famous knights

Some knights were famous for their bravery and fighting skills. Here are a few of them.

Richard I was a king who took part in the Crusades.

Saladin was a clever Muslim leader who fought the crusaders.

El Cid was a daring Spanish knight who never lost a battle.

Joan of Arc was a young woman who led the French army.

This painting shows Richard I in battle.
He was nicknamed 'Richard the Lionheart'
because he was so brave.

Some knights became so rich and famous
that they didn't need to fight any more.

King Arthur

Knights told stories about Arthur, a wise king who once ruled Britain. His knights were called the Knights of the Round Table.

This old painting shows King Arthur and his knights sitting at the Round Table.

1. In one tale, an evil prince kidnapped Arthur's wife.

2. Lancelot, one of Arthur's knights, went to find her.

3. He had to cross a bridge made of a sword to reach her.

4. He challenged the evil prince to a fight and won.

King Henry III loved the stories of Arthur so much that he had a round table made for himself.

Glossary of knight words

Here are some of the words in this book you might not know. This page tells you what they mean.

 page - a young boy who was starting to learn to be a knight.

 squire - a boy who worked for a knight and trained hard to be one himself.

 joust - a game where two knights tried to knock each other off their horses.

 lance - a long pole that was used as a weapon in battles and jousts.

 shield - a thick, wooden plate. Knights used shields to protect themselves.

 battering ram - a heavy tree trunk that was used to smash walls or doors.

 courtyard - a busy area inside the castle walls where people worked or played.

Websites to visit

If you have a computer, you can find out more about knights on the Internet. On the Usborne Quicklinks website there are links to four fun websites.

Website 1 - Print out knight and castle pictures to fill in.

Website 2 - Dress a knight for battle.

Website 3 - Take a tour through the rooms of a castle.

Website 4 - Test your jousting skills in a great game.

To visit these websites, go to **www.usborne-quicklinks.com** and type the keywords "beginners knights". Then click on the link for the website you want to visit. Before you use the Internet, look at the safety guidelines inside the back cover of this book and ask an adult to read them with you.

Many knights dressed like this 600 years ago.

Index

Acknowledgements

Photographic manipulation by Mike Wheatley • Illustration page 31 by Sergio

Photo credits
The publishers are grateful to the following for permission to reproduce material:

© akg-images 10, 27; © Ancient Art and Architecture Collection 22, 28; © Archivo Iconografico, S.A./CORBIS 9;
© Bettmann/CORBIS 4; © Bibliothèque nationale de France 1; © By permission of The British Library, Harley
4425 f.12 21, Egerton 1500 f.46 24; © Dynamic Graphics back cover; © England's Medieval Festival at
Herstmonceux Castle, East Sussex 12-13, 16-17; © English Heritage Events (Paul Lewis) 2-3; © Paul
Almasy/CORBIS 25; © Photo : Andrew P. Banjorinas, Armour : Christian Tobler 11; © Photo SCALA, Florence
(Pierpont Morgan Library) 7

Every effort has been made to trace and acknowledge ownership of copyright. If any rights have
been omitted, the publishers offer to rectify this in any subsequent editions following notification.